SEED SAVING
For beginners

Master Year-Round Seed Techniques, Comprehensive Guide for Harvesting, Storing, Germinating & Growing Diverse Seeds for Ultimate Self-Sufficiency, Perfect for Preppers & Home Gardeners. Essential for Sustainable Living

by Sophie G. Norring

" We do not inherit the Earth
from our ancestors,
but borrow it from our children "

SEED SAVING
For beginners

 Sophie G. Norring is a passionate author and expert gardener, shining brightly in the world of sustainable horticulture. Her deep love for nature and commitment to preserving the environment resonate through her writings, inspiring countless others to embrace the art of gardening. Sophie's journey, rich with hands-on experience and heartwarming encounters, empowers readers to cultivate not just their gardens, but also a greener future.

"Inspirational and Informative"
"Sophie's book isn't just informative, it's a source of inspiration. Her detailed guide on seed saving has opened my eyes to the wonders of gardening. Highly recommend it to anyone looking for a deeper connection with nature."

"Perfect for Beginners!"
"As a beginner in gardening, I was looking for something straightforward yet comprehensive. Sophie's book is exactly that! It's easy to understand, full of useful tips, and truly made me feel capable and excited about starting my garden!"

"Transformed My Garden"
"Sophie G. Norring's book has transformed my garden! The techniques for seed saving are clearly explained and easy to follow. My garden has never looked better, and I feel more eco-conscious. A must-read!"

"Truly Eye-Opening!"
"This book is a revelation! Sophie's approach to gardening and seed saving is both innovative and easy to adopt. It's changed the way I look at plants and my environmental impact. A must-have for every gardener."

"An Absolute Delight"
"I'm amazed at the wealth of knowledge in this book. Sophie G. Norring writes with such clarity and enthusiasm that you can't help but be drawn into the world of seed saving. It's an absolute delight for anyone interested in sustainable living."

"Just a Scan Away!"

Hey there, amazing reader! Loved diving into the world of seeds and gardening with our book?

Simply scan the QR code here

you can receive your fantastic BONUS

Thanks for being awesome! #SpreadTheGreenLove

TABLE OF CONTENT

Introduction

In a world where environmental concerns have taken center stage, the role of the modern gardener has evolved from a simple hobbyist to a guardian of green, embracing sustainable and environmentally friendly gardening practices. This transformation mirrors the increasing awareness of the consequences of human activities on the planet and the imperative to safeguard and conserve our natural environment.

The Rebirth of the Modern Gardener: From Simple Hobbyist to Guardian of Green in an Ever-Evolving World

In a world marked by rapid urbanization and environmental challenges, the role of the modern gardener has experienced a remarkable rebirth. What was once a simple hobby has evolved into a crucial responsibility: the guardians of green. This transformation is fueled by an expanding awareness of the significance of sustainable living and the necessity to conserve our natural world for the well-being of future generations.

The modern gardener is no longer just a casual hobbyist tending to a small plot of land. They have become stewards of our planet, taking on the role of environmental guardians. This transformation is underpinned by several key factors.

First and foremost, climate change has thrust the importance of sustainable living into the global spotlight. As extreme weather events, rising temperatures, and biodiversity loss continue to threaten our planet, individuals have recognized the need to take action. The modern gardener plays a pivotal role in combating these challenges by cultivating green spaces that not only provide beauty and solace but also help to mitigate the effects of climate change. From creating urban oases that combat heat island effects to planting native species that support local ecosystems, gardeners are on the front lines of environmental conservation.

Furthermore, the shift towards organic and eco-friendly practices has become a hallmark of the modern gardening movement. Traditional chemical-laden approaches are being replaced with methods that prioritize soil health, water conservation, and the overall well-being of the environment. Composting, mulching, and sustainable pest management techniques are just a few examples of how gardeners are adopting eco-conscious practices.

Technology has also played a significant role in the rebirth of the modern gardener. From smart irrigation systems that conserve water to apps that help with plant identification and care, technology has empowered gardeners with knowledge and tools to make informed decisions and optimize their green spaces.

Education and community involvement are essential components of this transformation. Modern gardeners are not operating in isolation; they are integral members of a global community that exchanges knowledge and experiences. Gardening clubs, online forums, and workshops have become hubs of learning and support.

A Guide to Sustainable and Environmentally Friendly Gardening

In this environmentally conscious era, eco-friendly gardening is crucial. Whether you're a beginner or a seasoned gardener, there are measures you can adopt to reduce your environmental footprint and establish a sustainable garden.

1. **Conscious Plant Selection:** Choose plants that are native to your area because they have already adapted to the weather and the soil there. Native plants typically demand less water and upkeep, given that they are already naturally adapted to the local environment. By choosing native species, you can help preserve local biodiversity and support the natural ecosystem of your region.

2. **Water Conservation:** Implement water-saving techniques such as drip irrigation and mulching. Drip irrigation directs water straight to the plant roots, reducing water wastage from evaporation and runoff. Mulching assists in retaining soil moisture and inhibiting weed growth, thus diminishing the requirement for excessive watering and chemical weed control.

3. **Composting and Natural Fertilizers:** Utilize composting to create nutrient-rich soil amendments for your garden. Compost not only enhances soil fertility but also lessens the reliance on synthetic fertilizers, which can have detrimental effects on the environment. Additionally, consider using natural fertilizers such as compost tea, bone meal, and seaweed extracts to promote plant growth without the negative environmental consequences associated with synthetic alternatives.

4. **Integrated Pest Management (IPM):** Employ IPM techniques to control pests and diseases in your garden without relying on harmful chemicals. This approach involves a combination of preventive measures, biological controls, and selective use of eco-friendly pesticides. By promoting natural predators and upholding a balanced ecosystem, you can efficiently control pests while minimizing any adverse effects on beneficial insects and the environment.

5. **Wildlife-Friendly Practices:** Create a welcoming habitat for local wildlife by incorporating native plants, bird feeders, and bee-friendly flowers in your garden. By offering food, shelter, and water sources, you can draw in beneficial insects, birds, and other wildlife that play a crucial role in maintaining the health and equilibrium of your garden ecosystem. It's essential to refrain from using pesticides that can harm these valuable garden allies.

6. **Rainwater Harvesting:** Installing a rainwater harvesting system enables you to gather and store rainwater for irrigation needs. By harnessing and utilizing rainwater, you can decrease dependency on municipal water sources and preserve this valuable resource. Rainwater is naturally free of the additives

commonly found in tap water, making it a healthier option for your plants and the environment.

7. **Natural Pest Deterrents:** Use natural deterrents, such as companion planting and physical barriers, to protect your garden from unwanted pests. Companion planting involves strategically placing certain plants together to repel pests or attract beneficial insects. Physical barriers, like netting and row covers, can serve as effective means to protect your plants without the need for chemical pesticides.

8. **Biodiversity Promotion:** Encourage biodiversity in your garden by creating a variety of habitats for different plant and animal species. Incorporate a mix of flowering plants, shrubs, and trees to provide food and shelter for a diverse range of wildlife. By fostering a rich and balanced ecosystem, you can help maintain a healthy and resilient garden environment.

9. **Energy-Efficient Tools and Equipment:** Choose energy-efficient and environmentally friendly tools and equipment for your gardening activities. Opt for hand tools or electric alternatives over gas-powered machinery to reduce your carbon footprint. Additionally, consider investing in solar-powered lighting and irrigation systems to minimize energy consumption and reliance on non-renewable resources.

10. **Educational Outreach:** Share your sustainable gardening practices with others in your community and encourage them to adopt similar environmentally friendly techniques. Arrange workshops, community garden initiatives, or educational events to increase awareness about the advantages of sustainable gardening and motivate others to make environmentally conscious decisions in their own gardens.

Interactive Space: Depicting the Ideal Garden

An ideal garden interactive space blends beauty, functionality, and sustainability. Here's how to make it happen:

1. **Native Plant Oasis:** The heart of the interactive garden is a thriving native plant oasis. It showcases the diverse flora of the region, educating visitors about the importance of native species in supporting local wildlife, conserving water, and enhancing biodiversity. The garden is organized into distinct zones, each representing a different local ecosystem.

2. **Educational Signage:** Throughout the garden, informative signage explains the significance of native plants, their role in local ecosystems, and their low-maintenance benefits. Visitors can learn how to identify these plants and the wildlife they attract, fostering a deeper appreciation for the environment.

3. **Pollinator Paradise:** A dedicated pollinator garden is designed to attract bees, butterflies, and other beneficial insects. Visitors can watch these pollinators at work, demonstrating the crucial role they play in food production. The interactive space includes a pollinator-friendly plant identification guide and showcases methods for creating pollinator-friendly habitats.

4. **Sustainable Gardening Practices:** A section of the garden demonstrates sustainable gardening techniques. Composting bins, rainwater harvesting systems, and eco-friendly fertilizers are on display. Visitors can learn how to reduce waste, conserve water, and use organic practices to nurture their own gardens while minimizing their ecological footprint.

5. **Edible Garden:** An edible garden showcases the beauty and practicality of growing food at home. Raised beds, vertical gardening, and container gardening are featured, making efficient use of limited space. Visitors can see how easy it is

to incorporate vegetables, herbs, and fruits into their landscape while reducing food miles and chemical exposure.

6. **Wildlife Observation Stations:** Hidden viewing areas equipped with binoculars and guides enable visitors to observe the wildlife that visits the garden. Bird feeders and water features attract avian visitors, while strategically placed nesting boxes provide safe havens for nesting birds. Encounters with local fauna bring a sense of connection to nature.

7. **Recycled Art Installations:** Sustainable art installations made from recycled materials add a creative touch to the garden. These sculptures, mosaics, and decorative elements emphasize the importance of repurposing and reusing materials to reduce waste and encourage sustainable design.

8. **Children's Learning Area:** A dedicated space for young gardeners offers hands-on experiences with planting and caring for native species, creating a fun and educational environment for children. Interactive exhibits, games, and gardening workshops make the garden a family-friendly destination that fosters a love for the outdoors.

9. **Community Engagement:** The interactive garden hosts community events, workshops, and garden clubs to connect like-minded individuals and provide a platform for sharing knowledge and ideas. It becomes a focal point for sustainability initiatives, where neighbors come together to discuss and implement eco-conscious gardening practices.

10. **Seasonal Exhibitions:** To keep the garden vibrant and evolving, seasonal exhibitions are featured. From spring bulb displays to summer butterfly gardens and fall harvest festivals, these exhibitions showcase the ever-changing beauty and opportunities for sustainable gardening throughout the year.

PART 1

The Magic of Seed Conservation

S eeds are the tiny capsules of life that hold within them the potential for a future filled with lush, green landscapes and bountiful harvests. The act of seed conservation is nothing short of magical, as it ensures the preservation of genetic diversity and the continuation of life on Earth.

Time Travel: A Brief History and Culture Behind Seed Conservation

In the intricate tapestry of our world's history and culture, the practice of seed conservation stands as a testament to humanity's ability to traverse time. This extraordinary endeavor, rooted in ancient traditions and continually evolving, allows us to protect the past and future of our planet's biodiversity. Seed conservation is not only an essential tool for ensuring food security but also a journey through time, connecting us with our agricultural heritage and preserving the genetic richness of our plant species.

Ancient Beginnings

The practice of seed saving has ancient origins, dating back thousands of years to the earliest human agricultural endeavors. In ancient civilizations such as Mesopotamia, China, and the Indus Valley, farmers intuitively recognized the value of collecting and replanting seeds from their best crops. This rudimentary form of seed conservation laid the groundwork for the future of agriculture.

Cultural Significance

Over time, the practice of seed saving evolved into a cultural tradition deeply intertwined with the identities of various communities around the world. For Indigenous peoples, seed saving is an integral part of their cultural heritage. The Native American Three Sisters planting method, for instance, showcases the synergy between corn, beans, and squash, demonstrating not only agricultural wisdom but also a profound understanding of biodiversity and sustainable agriculture.

Similarly, in Asia, rice varieties have been passed down through generations. The aromatic Basmati rice, for example, has been cultivated in the Indian subcontinent for centuries and is celebrated for its unique flavor and fragrance. The preservation of such traditional rice varieties not only maintains cultural identity but also ensures agricultural resilience and food security.

In Europe, seed saving was also integral to agrarian societies. Heirloom varieties of vegetables like tomatoes, cucumbers, and pumpkins were cherished for their taste and unique attributes, and the practice of saving seeds became a way for families to pass down their agricultural heritage.

The Green Revolution and the Decline of Diversity

The mid-20th century brought about significant changes in agricultural practices with the advent of the Green Revolution. This era was marked by the widespread adoption of high-yielding crop varieties, often at the expense of traditional and locally adapted seeds. While these new varieties increased food production, they also led to a decline in agricultural diversity as traditional and heirloom varieties were replaced.

The focus on a limited number of high-yielding crops contributed to the loss of many indigenous and locally adapted plant varieties. As a result, agricultural biodiversity was threatened, and the cultural significance of many traditional seed-saving practices began to wane.

The Modern Seed Conservation Movement

Recognizing the need to preserve biodiversity and the cultural significance of seed saving, the modern seed conservation movement emerged. Organizations and seed banks, such as the Svalbard Global Seed Vault in Norway and the Millennium Seed Bank in the United Kingdom, were established to collect, catalog, and safeguard seeds from around the world.

These initiatives aim to ensure that the genetic diversity of plant species is protected for future generations. In the face of climate change, emerging plant diseases, and the need for more sustainable agriculture, preserving a wide array of plant genetics is essential for food security and agricultural resilience.

Community Seed Banks and Reviving Traditions

While large-scale seed banks play a crucial role in seed conservation, community-based efforts are equally vital. Community seed banks, often run by local organizations and farmers, focus on preserving regional and heirloom varieties. These banks engage communities in seed saving, sharing knowledge, and celebrating the cultural significance of traditional seeds.

Furthermore, the concept of open-source seed sharing has gained momentum in recent years. Seed libraries and exchange networks enable individuals to share seeds freely, promoting the idea that seeds are a common heritage. This movement fosters a sense of community and encourages the revival of seed-saving traditions, connecting people to their agricultural roots.

The Global Seed Vault

The Svalbard Global Seed Vault, often referred to as the "Doomsday Vault," stands as an iconic symbol of the world's commitment to preserving agricultural biodiversity. Located deep within the Arctic permafrost, this secure facility houses over one million seed samples from across the globe. It serves as a global backup system, protecting the genetic diversity of our most vital crops.

The Global Seed Vault is a beacon of hope for humanity, offering a safeguard against unforeseen catastrophes, be they natural or man-made. It demonstrates our collective responsibility to ensure the legacy of seed conservation continues, allowing future generations to benefit from the genetic resources that have sustained life on our planet for millennia.

<u>Seed Conservation in the Face of Climate Change</u>

Climate change poses a significant challenge to seed conservation efforts. With rising temperatures and increasingly unpredictable weather patterns, the adaptability of plant species becomes of utmost importance. Seeds that have been conserved over time can serve as a reservoir of genetic traits, allowing us to breed new crop varieties that can withstand changing environmental conditions.

In the face of climate change, seed conservation takes on even greater significance. As we witness the displacement of agricultural zones and shifts in growing seasons, access to a diverse range of seeds with different traits becomes vital for ensuring food security and resilience in the agricultural sector.

The Green Legacy: Environmental, Economic Benefits, and Beyond

The practice of seed conservation, often hailed as the green legacy of our planet, holds significant importance far beyond preserving biodiversity. This endeavor offers various advantages, including environmental sustainability, food security, economic stability, and cultural preservation, fostering a more resilient, sustainable, and interconnected global society.

1. **Environmental Resilience and Biodiversity Preservation**

The core of seed conservation lies in environmental resilience and preserving biodiversity. It safeguards the genetic resources of numerous plant species, ensuring adaptability to changing environmental conditions, countering pests, diseases, and climate change. This genetic diversity supports the balance and health of ecosystems, benefiting both flora and fauna.

2. Sustainable Agriculture and Food Security

Seed conservation is pivotal for sustainable agriculture and global food security. Preserving diverse seed varieties enables agricultural resilience, reducing dependence on chemicals and enhancing sustainability. In the face of a growing global population and climate change challenges, it provides a safety net against crop failures, ensuring a stable food supply, particularly in volatile regions.

3. Economic Stability and Agricultural Innovation

Seed conservation contributes to economic stability and agricultural innovation. It encourages the development of new crop varieties with higher yields, improved nutrition, and pest resistance. This boosts productivity and creates economic opportunities while preserving cultural heritage and supporting local economies.

4. Scientific Advancements and Global Collaboration

The green legacy of seed conservation fuels scientific advancements and global collaboration. Seed banks and initiatives facilitate sharing genetic resources, driving innovative agricultural solutions and promoting international cooperation. This shared commitment fosters global unity and mutual responsibility for our planet's natural resources.

5. Educational and Community Engagement

Seed conservation serves as an educational platform and encourages community engagement. It offers opportunities to learn about biodiversity, sustainable agriculture, and environmental stewardship, fostering an understanding of ecosystem interconnectedness. Community involvement empowers individuals to become stewards of local biodiversity, promoting social cohesion and sustainability.

PART 2

Gardening 101 - Creating Your Green

Oasis

Embarking on the journey to create your own green oasis is an exciting endeavor that promises a deep connection with nature and the satisfaction of nurturing life. Whether you have a sprawling backyard or a modest balcony, the principles of sustainable gardening can be applied to any space, big or small.

The Blank Canvas: Choosing the Ideal Area for Your Sustainable Garden

Embarking on the journey to create a sustainable garden is an exciting endeavor, but the first step is perhaps the most crucial: selecting the ideal location for your green oasis. The chosen area will set the stage for your garden's success and its environmental impact. By considering key factors such as sunlight, soil quality, and access to water, you can transform your blank canvas into a flourishing and sustainable garden that benefits both the environment and your well-being.

<u>Sunlight</u>

Sunlight is the artist's paintbrush when it comes to gardening. It is the primary energy source that fuels photosynthesis, enabling plants to convert sunlight into food. Therefore, the first consideration in selecting a garden location is sunlight availability.

- **Assess Sunlight Patterns:** Observe the patterns of sunlight in your potential garden area. Most vegetables, flowers, and many herbs thrive with at least 6-8 hours of direct sunlight per day. Plants such as tomatoes, peppers, and sunflowers are considered "full sun" and require ample light to flourish. Shadier spots may be more suitable for plants like leafy greens, certain herbs, or shade-loving ornamental species.

- **Microclimates:** Be aware of microclimates within your garden area. Factors such as buildings, walls, and trees can create microclimates that influence temperature and sunlight. These microclimates can be advantageous if you aim to prolong your growing season or provide shade for specific plants.

<u>Soil Quality</u>

The next aspect to consider is the quality of the soil in your chosen area. Soil is the foundation upon which your garden will thrive, and its health is pivotal for sustainable gardening practices.

- **Conduct a Soil Test:** Before planting, it's advisable to conduct a soil test to assess its pH level, nutrient composition, and overall quality. You can purchase soil testing kits or consult with local agricultural extensions to obtain professional soil analysis. The results will guide you on any necessary amendments, such as adding organic matter to improve soil structure or adjusting pH levels.
- **Drainage:** Evaluate the soil's drainage capacity. Well-draining soil prevents waterlogged roots and reduces the risk of root rot. If your garden area has poor drainage, consider raised beds or incorporating organic matter to improve soil aeration.

<u>Water Source</u>

Access to water is a crucial aspect of sustainable gardening. Water conservation is not only an environmental responsibility but also a practical consideration for maintaining a thriving garden.

- **Proximity to Water:** Choose a garden location that is close to a water source, such as a rain barrel, garden hose, or irrigation system. This will make watering more convenient and efficient.
- **Consider Rainfall Patterns:** Take into account your region's average rainfall patterns. If you live in an area with frequent rainfall, you may need less irrigation, while in drier climates, you may need to invest in water-efficient irrigation systems or drought-tolerant plant varieties.
- **Rainwater Harvesting:** Embrace sustainable practices like rainwater harvesting. Collecting rainwater in barrels or cisterns can provide an eco-friendly

water source for your garden, reducing the need for municipal water and conserving this precious resource.

<u>Accessibility and Convenience</u>

The convenience and accessibility of your garden area play a vital role in your gardening experience and sustainability efforts.

- **Proximity to the Home:** Consider the proximity of your garden to your home. A garden that is closer to your living space is more likely to be regularly tended to and monitored for pests, diseases, and watering needs.
- **Accessibility for Maintenance:** Ensure that your garden area is accessible for maintenance tasks, including weeding, harvesting, and soil amendments. Paths or walkways can make it easier to navigate through the garden without compacting the soil.
- **Safety and Visibility:** Keep safety and visibility in mind, especially if you have children or pets. Choose a garden location that allows for clear sightlines to supervise outdoor activities while also considering potential safety hazards, such as poisonous plants.

<u>Environmental Considerations</u>

Sustainable gardening is, by its very nature, harmonious with the environment. When choosing your garden area, consider how it aligns with ecological principles.

- **Native Plant Integration:** If possible, consider incorporating native plant species into your garden design. Native plants are well-suited to local conditions, demanding less water and maintenance, while also offering crucial habitat and food sources for native wildlife.
- **Wildlife-Friendly Features:** Create wildlife-friendly features in your garden, such as bird feeders, butterfly gardens, or small water features. These elements enhance the ecological value of your garden and encourage biodiversity.
- **Environmental Impact:** Assess the potential environmental impact of your garden area. Avoid locations that may disrupt natural habitats or contribute to soil erosion. Instead, aim to enhance the surrounding ecosystem by choosing sustainable planting options.

Essential Tools to Begin

Starting a gardening journey can be a rewarding and enriching experience. Whether you're looking to cultivate beautiful flowers, grow your own food, or create a sustainable oasis, having the right tools is crucial for your success. Here, we'll explore the essential tools every beginner gardener should consider to get started on the right foot.

1. **Hand Trowel**

A hand trowel is one of the most versatile and essential tools for any gardener. This compact, handheld tool is ideal for tasks such as digging, transplanting, weeding, and making holes for small plants and bulbs. Look for a trowel with a comfortable handle and a durable, rust-resistant blade to make your gardening tasks more efficient.

2. **Pruners or Secateurs**

Pruners, also known as secateurs, are used for cutting stems, branches, and dead growth on your plants. They come in various styles, including bypass pruners (which work like scissors) and anvil pruners (which have a blade that cuts against a flat surface). Select a style that aligns with your requirements and invest in a top-quality pair for precise, clean cuts that enhance plant health.

3. **Garden Gloves**

Garden gloves are essential for keeping your hands clean and protected while working in the garden. They shield your skin from dirt, thorns, and potential irritants. Look for gloves that fit well and provide good grip while allowing for dexterity to handle various gardening tasks.

4. **Garden Fork**

A garden fork is a valuable tool for turning and loosening soil, breaking up clumps, and incorporating compost or other soil amendments. It's essential for preparing your garden beds, improving soil aeration, and promoting healthy root growth.

5. Rake

A rake is crucial for leveling soil, spreading mulch, removing leaves, and keeping your garden tidy. Invest in a durable garden rake with adjustable tines, which allows you to adapt the tool to different garden tasks.

6. Watering Can or Hose

Proper watering is essential for plant health, so having a reliable watering can or hose is a must. A watering can is perfect for smaller gardens or potted plants, while a garden hose is suitable for larger spaces. Look for a hose with an adjustable nozzle for control over water flow.

7. Wheelbarrow or Garden Cart

A wheelbarrow or garden cart is invaluable for transporting soil, mulch, plants, and heavy gardening materials. It reduces strain on your back and makes tasks like moving compost or mulch much more manageable.

8. Soil pH Tester

Understanding your soil's pH level is crucial for successful gardening. A soil pH tester, typically available as a handheld probe or meter, aids in assessing whether your soil is acidic, neutral, or alkaline. Understanding your soil's pH enables you to select plants that will flourish in your garden and make informed choices about soil amendments.

9. Garden Pruner Sharpener

Keeping your pruners, shears, and other cutting tools sharp is essential for clean and healthy cuts. A garden pruner sharpener is a convenient tool that ensures your cutting equipment stays in optimal condition. Regular maintenance prolongs the lifespan of your tools and helps prevent damage to your plants.

10. Garden Kneeler/Seat

Gardening can be physically demanding, so a garden kneeler/seat provides comfort and support. It's a versatile tool that allows you to kneel or sit while gardening, reducing strain on your knees and back. Some models even come with built-in pockets for carrying tools and supplies.

11. Garden Shears or Hedge Trimmers

If you have hedges or shrubs in your garden, a good pair of garden shears or hedge trimmers is essential for shaping and maintaining their appearance. They make pruning and trimming tasks more efficient and help keep your landscape looking neat and well-maintained.

12. Garden Weeder

Weeding is a necessary chore in any garden. A garden weeder, often with a forked or hooked end, helps you remove weeds from the soil with minimal disturbance to your desired plants. Choose one that suits your specific weeding needs, whether for large garden beds or tight spaces.

13. Garden Apron or Tool Belt

A garden apron or tool belt is a handy accessory that keeps your essential tools within easy reach. It's particularly helpful when you're moving around your garden, planting, and performing various tasks. Look for one with pockets and compartments for storing trowels, pruners, and other small tools.

14. Garden Shovel

A garden shovel is essential for digging holes for planting, moving soil, and transplanting larger plants. Look for a sturdy and well-balanced shovel with a comfortable grip to make your digging tasks more manageable.

15. Garden Twine or String

Garden twine or string is a versatile tool for staking plants, creating trellises, and organizing your garden. It helps support climbing plants, keep rows straight, and secure plants to prevent wind damage.

PART 3

Choose with Heart - Discover and Select Your Green Gems

In the pursuit of a vibrant and thriving garden, selecting the right plants is paramount. This section will guide you through the process of discovering and choosing green gems that not only contribute to the beauty of your garden but also play a crucial role in seed conservation efforts. Additionally, we will delve into the essential practices of identifying healthy plants and recognizing those that may pose risks to your garden's overall well-being.

Selecting Plants for Seed Conservation

Seed conservation is a critical practice for preserving biodiversity, ensuring food security, and promoting sustainable gardening. Selecting the right plants for seed conservation is a crucial step in this process. Whether you're interested in saving seeds from food crops, ornamental plants, or native species, understanding the criteria and techniques for plant selection is essential.

1. **Genetic Diversity**

Genetic diversity is the cornerstone of seed conservation. To select plants for conservation, it's essential to prioritize species or varieties that represent a broad genetic pool. A diverse gene pool helps plants adapt to changing environmental conditions and resist pests and diseases.

- **Choose Heirloom and Open-Pollinated Varieties:** Heirloom plants and open-pollinated varieties are excellent choices for seed conservation because they tend to maintain genetic diversity. These plants have often been cultivated for generations, making them valuable reservoirs of genetic information.
- **Local and Indigenous Species:** Native and indigenous plant species are adapted to local climates and soil conditions. They often possess unique genetic traits that make them valuable for seed conservation. By prioritizing these species, you support the preservation of regional biodiversity.

2. Plant Health and Vigor

Healthy, vigorous plants are more likely to produce high-quality seeds. When selecting plants for seed conservation, prioritize those that exhibit robust growth, disease resistance, and pest tolerance. Here are some key considerations:

- **Observation and Selection:** Monitor the plants in your garden or conservation area throughout the growing season. Select seeds from the healthiest and most vigorous individuals that exhibit desirable traits.
- **Avoid Disease-Prone Plants:** Plants that are consistently affected by diseases may pass on those vulnerabilities to their offspring. Be cautious when saving seeds from plants with a history of disease issues.

3. Pollination Methods

Understanding the pollination methods of the plants you want to conserve is crucial. Different pollination methods impact how seeds are saved and maintained.

- **Self-Pollinated Plants:** Self-pollinating plants, such as beans and tomatoes, are typically easier to save seeds from. They have a higher degree of genetic consistency since they primarily fertilize themselves. To prevent cross-pollination, isolate self-pollinated plants from other varieties of the same species.
- **Cross-Pollinated Plants:** Cross-pollinated plants, like cucumbers and corn, require more meticulous isolation techniques. To maintain their genetic purity, you need to prevent cross-pollination with other varieties of the same species, often through physical barriers like distance or time separation.

4. Planting Space and Isolation

Maintaining genetic purity is crucial for seed conservation. Cross-pollination between different varieties can result in hybrid seeds, compromising the integrity of the conserved variety. Here's how to prevent cross-pollination:

- **Spatial Isolation:** Plant different varieties of the same species at a considerable distance apart. This physical separation minimizes the chances of cross-pollination by wind, insects, or other pollinators.
- **Time Isolation:** Some plants can be separated by their flowering times to avoid cross-pollination. Planting early and late varieties of the same species can help prevent genetic mixing.
- **Hand Pollination:** For plants where isolation isn't feasible, consider hand-pollination. This involves manually transferring pollen from one flower to another to control pollination and maintain genetic purity.

5. **Disease Resistance and Tolerance**

Selecting plants with a history of disease resistance or tolerance is beneficial for both your garden's health and seed conservation. Disease-resistant plants are more likely to produce healthy seeds that can withstand common garden challenges.

- **Variety Research:** Before selecting a plant for conservation, research its disease resistance traits. Varieties bred for resistance to specific diseases can contribute to your garden's overall health and longevity.

6. **Adaptable and Climate-Resilient Plants**

Climate change poses significant challenges to gardeners. When selecting plants for seed conservation, consider those that are adaptable to changing weather patterns, temperature fluctuations, and unpredictable growing conditions.

- **Local Adaptation:** Choose plants that are known to thrive in your specific climate. They have likely developed genetic traits that help them withstand local weather extremes and seasonal fluctuations.
- **Crop Wild Relatives:** Investigate crop wild relatives, which are often more adaptable and resilient. These plants can be sources of valuable genetic material for breeding programs and future conservation efforts.

7. **Record Keeping**

Accurate record-keeping is essential for successful seed conservation. Keeping detailed records of the plants you're conserving will help you track the history and performance of each variety.

- **Data to Record:** Document the variety, source, planting date, and any specific traits or characteristics of the plants you're conserving. Note any changes or adaptations observed in the plants over time.
- **Labeling and Organization:** Use clear and durable labels to tag each plant or variety. Organize your records to ensure you can trace the history and performance of the seeds you're saving.

8. Seed Harvesting and Storage

Proper seed harvesting and storage are critical to maintain seed viability over time. Learn the techniques for harvesting and storing seeds from different plant species to ensure their long-term preservation.

- **Dry and Store Seeds:** After harvesting seeds, ensure they are thoroughly dried to prevent mold and disease. Store seeds in airtight containers in a cool, dark, and dry location. Include moisture-absorbing packets to reduce humidity levels within storage containers.
- **Regular Viability Testing:** Periodically test the viability of your stored seeds to ensure they remain viable. If necessary, refresh your seed collection by sowing and saving seeds from the resulting plants.

9. Sustainable Practices

Sustainable gardening practices extend to seed conservation efforts. As you embark on your seed-saving journey, consider ethical and sustainable practices, such as the following:

- **Avoid Overharvesting:** When saving seeds from wild or native plants, avoid overharvesting to ensure their long-term survival in natural habitats.
- **Promote Open-Pollination:** Encourage open-pollination and genetic diversity within your garden. Open-pollinated plants create diverse gene pools that can benefit future conservation efforts.
- **Community Involvement:** Collaborate with local gardening communities or seed-saving organizations to exchange knowledge, seeds, and resources. Collective efforts can contribute to a broader range of conserved plant varieties.

10.   Sharing and Preservation

Seed conservation is not only about safeguarding seeds for your personal use but also about preserving and sharing plant varieties with the wider community. Consider the following steps:

- **Community Seed Libraries:** Support or establish community seed libraries to exchange and share seeds with fellow gardeners. These initiatives promote local biodiversity and conservation efforts.
- **Collaboration with Seed Banks:** Explore collaborations with seed banks and organizations that focus on preserving and sharing plant genetic diversity on a larger scale.
- **Educational Outreach:** Educate others about the importance of seed conservation and encourage them to participate in preserving plant varieties.

Identifying Healthy Plants and Those to Avoid

Creating a thriving garden begins with the selection of healthy plants and a cautious approach to those that may bring problems. When you can recognize the signs of a vigorous, disease-free plant versus one that's potentially problematic, you'll be well on your way to a garden that flourishes.

Identifying Healthy Plants

1. **Strong Roots**

Healthy plants often have strong root systems. When purchasing potted plants, gently slide the plant out of its pot to inspect the roots. Look for white or light-colored, firm, and well-branched roots. Avoid plants with brown or mushy roots, as they may be suffering from root rot or other diseases.

2. **Vibrant Foliage**

Healthy plants boast lush and vibrant foliage. Leaves should be green, unless the plant naturally has a different color, and free from discoloration, spots, or holes. Signs of healthy leaves include turgidity, uniform color, and a glossy appearance.

3. **No Signs of Pests**

Inspect plants for any visible signs of pests, such as chewed leaves, sticky residue (honeydew), or the presence of bugs. Healthy plants are typically pest-free, so avoid those with any visible infestations.

4. Disease-Free Appearance

Healthy plants should be free from visible signs of diseases, such as wilting, rotting, or mold. Be especially cautious of plants with dark spots, lesions, or strange growths, as these may be indicators of fungal or bacterial infections.

5. Balanced Growth

Healthy plants display balanced growth, with no excessive leggy stems, elongated internodes, or stunted growth. Look for compact, bushy plants with well-proportioned foliage.

6. Healthy Stems

Examine the stems for any signs of disease or damage. Healthy stems are firm and free from wounds, cankers, or discoloration. Avoid plants with soft or discolored stems, as these may be struggling or infected.

7. Free-Flowing Sap

Healthy plants should produce clear, clean sap when cut or pruned. If you observe discolored, foul-smelling, or oozing sap, it may indicate a problem within the plant.

8. Strong Aroma (for herbs and aromatic plants)

Plants like herbs and aromatic species should have a strong, characteristic aroma. Gently rub a leaf or stem between your fingers and take note of the scent. A robust, pleasant aroma is indicative of a healthy plant.

Identifying Plants to Avoid

1. Signs of Disease

Plants that exhibit visible signs of disease, such as wilting, mold, or discolored foliage, should be avoided. These symptoms can indicate an unhealthy plant that may introduce diseases to your garden.

2. Weak or Leggy Growth

Plants with weak, leggy growth may struggle to thrive in your garden. They often lack the vigor and energy needed to withstand pests and environmental stressors.

3. Pests or Pest Damage

Plants that show signs of pest infestations or have visible damage caused by insects should be avoided. Pests can swiftly propagate to other plants in your garden.

4. Overcrowding or Poor Spacing

If plants are overcrowded in their pots or planting beds, they may have to compete for resources like light, nutrients, and water. This competition can lead to stunted growth and decreased vitality.

5. Discolored or Wilted Foliage

Plants with discolored or wilting foliage may be under stress or suffering from diseases. Avoid plants with yellowing, brown, or drooping leaves, as they may not recover easily.

6. Poor Root Systems

Plants with weak or crowded root systems in their pots are more likely to struggle when transplanted. Avoid plants with root-bound or poorly developed roots.

7. Weak or Damaged Stems

Plants with weak, damaged, or discolored stems may have structural problems that affect their overall health and growth. Avoid these plants to prevent future issues.

8. Unpleasant Odor (for herbs and aromatic plants)

Some plants may emit an unpleasant or musty odor when crushed or bruised. This can be an indicator of disease or a state of poor health. Avoid plants with foul or unusual scents.

9. Unhealthy Soil

When purchasing potted plants, check the soil in the container. Soil that smells foul, is overly wet, or contains visible signs of mold or fungal growth is an indicator of an unhealthy plant.

10.   Non-Indigenous or Invasive Species

Plants that are not native to your region may require excessive care and maintenance to thrive. They can also become invasive and harm local ecosystems. Avoid planting non-indigenous or invasive species unless you are committed to managing them carefully.

11. Overly Mature or Leggy Transplants

Plants that are too mature or leggy may not adapt well to transplanting. They may have difficulty adjusting to new garden conditions and may take longer to establish themselves.

12. Poorly Labeled or Misidentified Plants

Always be cautious when purchasing plants that are mislabeled or have unclear identification. Properly labeled plants ensure you know what you're getting and that they're suitable for your garden.

PART 4

The Magical Moment - Seed Collection

Seed collection is a pivotal moment in the journey of nurturing your garden and contributing to seed conservation efforts. This section will transport you to the magical world of seed harvesting, where you will learn how to recognize the right moments for collection, understand nature's signals, and master the techniques and tools needed to gather seeds effectively.

Waiting for the Right Moment: Nature's Harvesting Signals

Nature provides us with a wealth of delicious, nutritious, and sustainable food, but harvesting the bounty of the natural world requires patience and a keen understanding of the signs and signals it offers. Whether you're foraging in the wild, tending to a garden, or picking fruit from trees, learning to recognize these cues is essential for knowing when the moment is just right to gather your harvest.

1. **Color Transformation**

One of the most straightforward indicators of readiness for harvesting is a change in color. Many fruits, vegetables, and even nuts undergo a transformation in color as they ripen. Here are a few examples:

- **Fruit Ripening:** Fruits like tomatoes, strawberries, and bananas turn vibrant red or yellow when they are ripe and ready to be picked. Others, like avocados, change from green to a dark purplish-black. Observing the color shift is a clear sign that the fruit is ready for harvest.

- **Leafy Greens:** Leafy vegetables, such as lettuce & spinach, are typically harvested when their leaves are tender, young, and vibrant green. Once they start to yellow or become tough and bitter, they are past their prime.

2. Aroma and Fragrance

The aroma of a plant can be an excellent indicator of readiness. Many fruits, herbs, and vegetables emit a distinctive fragrance when they are at their peak. For example:

- **Herbs:** Herbs like basil, mint, and cilantro release a strong, aromatic scent when they are ready to be picked. The aroma intensifies as the oils within the leaves become more concentrated.
- **Fruits:** Fruits like melons, peaches, and pineapples emit a sweet, fragrant odor when fully ripe. If you can smell the fruit's natural scent, it's usually a good sign that it's ready to harvest.

3. Texture and Firmness

The texture and firmness of a plant can offer valuable clues about its readiness for harvest:

- **Softness:** Many fruits, like peaches, plums, and tomatoes, are ready for harvest when they yield slightly to gentle pressure. If they feel too hard, they are underripe, and if they're mushy, they may be overripe.
- **Crispness:** Vegetables such as cucumbers and snap peas should have a crisp, taut texture when they are at their peak. When they become limp or rubbery, they are past their prime.

4. Sound and Audible Cues

Some plants provide audible cues to signal their readiness for harvest:

- **Audible "Pops":** Popcorn, as the name suggests, produces an audible "pop" when the kernels are ready to harvest. This happens when the moisture inside the kernel turns to steam, causing it to burst open.
- **Crackling Seeds:** Certain seeds, like sunflowers and beans, produce a crackling or rustling sound when they are dry and ready to be harvested.

5. Seed Dispersal

For plants that produce seeds, their method of seed dispersal can be a clear indication of when it's time to harvest:

- **Dandelions:** Dandelion seeds are attached to fluffy, white pappus (the "parachutes" attached to the seeds) that helps them float away in the wind. When the pappus is fully formed, it's a sign that the seeds are mature and ready for collection.
- **Dry Seed Heads:** Many plants, like basil or cilantro, produce seed heads that turn brown and dry as they mature. When these heads are ready to shatter and release their seeds, it's time to harvest them.

6. Taste Testing

In some cases, the best way to confirm that a plant is ready for harvest is to taste it. This is particularly true for fruits and vegetables. For example:

- **Berries:** Many berries, such as blueberries and blackberries, are at their sweetest and most flavorful when they are fully ripe. Taste-testing is often the most reliable method for determining their readiness.
- **Root Vegetables:** Root vegetables like carrots & beets can be dug up and tasted to gauge their sweetness and tenderness. If they taste good, they're ready to be harvested.

7. Visual and Audible Clues in the Wild

Foraging in the wild requires a keen eye and an understanding of natural cues. Here are some additional signals to look for:

- **Seeds on the Ground:** When you observe seeds or nuts on the ground near a tree or plant, it's a sign that they are likely mature and ready for harvesting. Squirrels and other wildlife are excellent foragers and can provide insight into the timing of a plant's maturity.
- **Bird Activity:** Birds are also skilled foragers and can clue you in on the readiness of certain fruits. If you notice birds flocking to a tree or bush, it's a good sign that the fruits are ripe.

8. Patience and Observation

Sometimes, nature's signals are subtle, and it takes time and close observation to determine the right moment for harvesting. For example:

- **Pomegranates:** Pomegranates are ready for harvest when the skin turns a rich, deep red, and the fruit feels heavy for its size. However, the best way to confirm readiness is by cutting a fruit open and examining the seeds. They should be plump and juicy, not dry or pale.
- **Edible Mushrooms:** Foragers should have a deep understanding of the specific species they are harvesting, as mushrooms have unique signs of maturity and are not always obvious. Gills, spore color, and cap size are all critical indicators.

9. **Local Wisdom and Seasonal Timing**

In many regions, local knowledge and traditions play a vital role in determining the right time for harvesting. People who have lived in a specific area for generations often have valuable insights into the seasonal cues and local wisdom related to harvesting.

10.   **Sustainability and Respect for Nature**

While it's essential to learn the signs and signals of readiness for harvesting, it's equally important to do so with respect and sustainability in mind. Overharvesting or disrupting natural ecosystems can harm the environment and future foraging opportunities.

Techniques and Tools for Effective Collection

Collecting plants, whether foraging in the wild or harvesting from your garden, requires a combination of techniques and tools to ensure success. Proper collection techniques not only maximize the yield but also promote sustainability and reduce harm to the environment.

Foraging in the Wild

Foraging involves gathering edible or useful plants from natural environments. To do this ethically and effectively, consider the following techniques and tools:

1. **Plant Identification**

Before you collect any plant, it's crucial to accurately identify it. Mistakenly gathering toxic plants can be dangerous, so invest in field guides, apps, or consult with experts to develop your identification skills. Always be 100% sure about a plant's identity before harvesting.

2. Sustainable Harvesting

Sustainability is key in foraging. Follow these guidelines to ensure you leave minimal impact:

- **Take Only What You Need:** Harvest only what you can use, and avoid collecting plants that are rare or vulnerable. Leave the majority of the population intact to ensure the plant's survival.
- **Use Scissors or Pruners:** When harvesting wild plants, use scissors or pruners to cut the plant cleanly, minimizing damage to the roots and surrounding vegetation.
- **Avoid Overharvesting:** Do not pick every plant of a species you encounter. Leave some behind to allow the population to regenerate.

3. Harvesting Tools for Wild Foraging

Carry the right tools to ensure effective and sustainable harvesting:

- **Scissors or Pruners:** These tools allow precise cuts without damaging the plant.
- **Small Basket or Bag:** A lightweight container for collecting your harvest without crushing the plants.
- **Field Guide or Smartphone App:** For plant identification in the field.
- **Gloves:** To protect your hands from thorns, stinging plants, or irritants.

Gardening and Cultivation

Harvesting from your garden or cultivated plants requires specific techniques and tools for efficient collection. Here are some key considerations:

1. Proper Timing

Timing is essential for harvesting garden crops. Different plants have different stages of maturity when they are at their peak for taste and quality. Here are a few examples:

- **Tomatoes:** Harvest when they are fully ripe, as indicated by their vibrant color and slight softness when gently squeezed.
- **Herbs:** Harvest leafy herbs like basil and cilantro just before they flower for the most intense flavor.

- **Root Vegetables:** Dig up root vegetables like carrots and potatoes when they have reached the desired size but before they become overgrown.

2. Harvesting Tools for Gardening

Having the right tools makes harvesting more efficient and less damaging to your plants:

- **Pruners or Shears:** For clean cuts on stems, branches, or larger fruits.
- **Hand Trowel or Shovel:** To carefully dig up root vegetables and other crops.
- **Harvesting Knife or Scissors:** Ideal for delicate crops like lettuce or herbs.
- **Picking Baskets or Containers:** To collect and transport your harvest without causing damage.

3. Proper Handling

Once you've harvested your garden crops, handling them carefully is essential to maintain their quality:

- **Handle with Care:** Treat your plants gently to avoid bruising or damage. For fruits and vegetables, use padded containers to prevent them from getting squashed or damaged during transport.
- **Keep it Clean:** Ensure your hands, tools, and containers are clean to prevent contamination and the spread of pathogens.

4. Sustainable Gardening Practices

Gardening practices can also promote sustainability in the garden:

- **Crop Rotation:** To prevent soil depletion & pest build-up, rotate crops annually.
- **Composting:** Recycle plant waste by turning it into compost, enriching your soil for future crops.
- **Water Management:** Use efficient watering techniques, like drip irrigation, to conserve water and reduce waste.

5. Seed Saving

For gardeners interested in sustainable practices, saving seeds is an essential technique:

- **Selecting Healthy Plants:** Save seeds from the healthiest, most vigorous plants that exhibit desirable traits.

- **Proper Drying and Storage:** Ensure that seeds are fully dry before storing them in a cool, dark, and dry place.
- **Record Keeping:** Maintain clear records of the seeds you save, including variety, source, and any specific traits.
- **Pollination Management:** To prevent cross-pollination and maintain seed purity, implement isolation techniques when saving seeds from cross-pollinated plants.

6. Continuous Monitoring

In both foraging and gardening, continuous monitoring is key:

- **Watch for Pests & Diseases:** Check your plants on a regular basis for any signs of disease or damage caused by pests. Early discovery makes it possible to take preventative measures against infestations as well as the spread of disease.
- **Check Maturity:** Monitor the maturity of your plants, so you harvest them at the right time. Some fruits and vegetables can ripen rapidly, and missing the optimal harvest window can result in a loss of quality.

7. Ethical Considerations

Whether you're foraging in the wild or harvesting from your garden, ethical considerations are crucial:

- **Leave No Trace:** When foraging in the wild, leave nature as you found it. Avoid trampling plants or disturbing wildlife.
- **Protect Pollinators:** In your garden, create a pollinator-friendly environment to support bees and other beneficial insects. Avoid the use of harmful pesticides.
- **Biodiversity:** In both foraging and gardening, promote biodiversity. Grow a variety of plant species to support ecological health and food diversity.

8. Sharing and Community

Both foragers and gardeners can benefit from sharing knowledge and experiences:

- **Foragers' Groups:** Join local foragers' groups to exchange information about prime foraging locations and plant identification.
- **Community Gardening:** Collaborate with community gardening organizations to share gardening knowledge and resources.

PART 5

Treasures in a Box - Conservation and Care

O nce you've experienced the magical moment of seed collection and gathered the fruits of your gardening efforts, it's time to safeguard these treasures in a box, ensuring the preservation of their vitality and genetic diversity. This section will guide you through the post-harvest routine, including the crucial steps of cleaning, drying, and storing seeds, and reveal the secrets to maintaining their long-term vitality.

Post-Harvest Routine: Cleaning, Drying, and Storing Seeds

Once you've successfully harvested seeds from your garden or foraged them from the wild, the next crucial step is to ensure their long-term viability by properly cleaning, drying, and storing them. Proper post-harvest care not only maintains the quality of the seeds but also extends their shelf life.

Cleaning Seeds

Cleaning seeds is the first step in the post-harvest routine. It removes any remaining plant material, debris, or contaminants from the seeds. This not only improves seed storage but also reduces the risk of pathogens or mold developing on the seeds. Here's how to clean seeds effectively:

Supplies You'll Need:

- A sieve or strainer with different-sized screens to separate seeds from debris.
- A shallow dish or tray for sorting seeds.
- A bucket or container for holding the seeds.
- Clean water for rinsing.

Steps for Cleaning Seeds:

1. **Collect Seeds:** Start by gathering the seeds you wish to clean. These can be seeds from harvested fruits, vegetables, herbs, or foraged plants.

2. **Remove Excess Debris:** Initially, pick out any large debris like leaves, stems, or twigs by hand. A gentle shake or tapping the plant material over a tray can help dislodge seeds.

3. **Rinse Seeds:** In some cases, rinsing seeds can be helpful. Submerge the seeds in clean, cool water, and use your fingers to gently rub the seeds and separate them from clinging debris.

4. **Use a Sieve:** To further separate seeds from plant material, pass them through a sieve or strainer. Select a sieve with the appropriate-sized mesh to allow seeds to pass through while trapping larger debris.

5. **Sort Seeds:** After sieving, transfer the seeds to a shallow dish or tray. Inspect them carefully for any remaining plant material, and remove it by hand.

Drying Seeds

Drying is a critical step to reduce the moisture content in seeds, which is crucial for preventing mold and maintaining seed viability. The drying process should be conducted with care to prevent any damage to the seeds. Here's how to dry seeds effectively:

Supplies You'll Need:

- A tray, plate, or dish for spreading seeds in a single layer.
- A well-ventilated, dry, and dark area.

Steps for Drying Seeds:

1. **Spread Seeds in a Single Layer:** After cleaning, spread the seeds in a single layer on a tray, plate, or dish. This ensures even drying and prevents seeds from clumping together.

2. **Choose a Suitable Location:** Place the tray in a well-ventilated area, away from direct sunlight, in a dry and dark environment. The seeds should be protected from moisture and humidity.

3. **Allow Adequate Time:** The drying process can take anywhere from a few days to a few weeks, depending on the seeds' size and moisture content. Be patient and ensure that the seeds are completely dry before proceeding to the next step.

4. **Test for Dryness:** To check if the seeds are dry, squeeze a few seeds between your thumb and forefinger. If they feel hard, brittle, and don't bend, they are adequately dried.

Storing Seeds

Storing seeds properly is the key to maintaining their viability and ensuring successful germination in the future. The goal is to protect the seeds from moisture, pests, and temperature fluctuations. Follow these steps for storing seeds:

Supplies You'll Need:

- Small, airtight containers or seed envelopes.
- Silica gel packets or rice for moisture control.
- A cool, dark, and dry storage location.

Steps for Storing Seeds:

1. **Use Appropriate Containers:** Transfer the fully dried seeds to small, airtight containers, like glass jars, or seed envelopes. Make sure the containers are clean and dry.

2. **Label the Containers:** Label each container with the name of the seed variety and the date it was harvested. This helps you keep track of the seeds and their age.

3. **Add Moisture Control:** To prevent moisture buildup within the containers, include moisture-absorbing packets or place a few grains of rice in a cloth bag. These help maintain the seeds' moisture content at an appropriate level.

4. **Store in a Cool, Dark, and Dry Place:** Choose a cool, dark, and dry location for storing seeds. A basement, pantry, or refrigerator can be suitable. Avoid exposing seeds to direct sunlight or temperature fluctuations.

5. **Regularly Check Seeds:** Periodically check your stored seeds for signs of moisture or pests. If you notice any issues, address them immediately to ensure the seeds remain in good condition.

Additional Tips for Successful Seed Storage:

- **Use Airtight Containers:** Airtight containers are crucial for preventing moisture and pests from infiltrating your seed storage.
- **Optimal Temperature:** Store seeds at temperatures around 40°F (4°C) or slightly cooler. This helps maintain their viability.
- **Avoid Freezing:** While cooler temperatures are ideal, avoid freezing seeds, as it can damage them.
- **Test Germination:** Periodically test the germination rate of stored seeds to ensure their viability. To do this, place a few seeds in a damp paper towel and observe their germination rate over a week.
- **Rotate Seeds:** To maintain seed viability, rotate your stored seeds by using the oldest ones first and replacing them with freshly harvested seeds.
- **Maintain Records:** Keep detailed records of your seed storage, including the seed varieties, dates, and conditions, to help you track seed longevity and viability.
- **Share Your Seeds:** Consider sharing your seeds with local seed libraries or gardening communities to promote biodiversity and seed-saving efforts.

Secrets to Preserving Seed Vitality

Seeds are the lifeblood of a sustainable garden, and their vitality is paramount for successful gardening endeavors. Preserving seed vitality ensures that your garden continues to thrive and provide bountiful harvests year after year.

1. **Select Healthy Plants**

The first secret to preserving seed vitality is to start with healthy plants. By choosing robust, disease-resistant, and well-adapted plant varieties, you lay the groundwork for strong and vital seeds. Here's how to do it:

- **Choose Open-Pollinated Varieties:** Select open-pollinated or heirloom plant varieties whenever possible. These plants tend to produce seeds with genetic diversity and adaptability.
- **Avoid Inbred or Weak Plants:** Be selective in your breeding choices, avoiding plants that show signs of inbreeding depression, disease susceptibility, or weakness.

2. **Isolate Crops for Pure Seeds**

Cross-pollination can lead to hybridization and reduce seed purity. To preserve seed vitality and maintain the characteristics of specific plant varieties, it's crucial to prevent cross-pollination. Here's how to achieve that:

- **Plant Separation:** Plant different varieties of the same species as far apart as their specific pollination needs require. Consult reliable sources for recommended isolation distances.
- **Hand-Pollination:** In some cases, you can manually pollinate plants to ensure pure seed production. Use small paintbrushes or cotton swabs to transfer pollen between flowers.
- **Time-Based Planting:** Stagger the planting times of related varieties to minimize the chances of them flowering simultaneously.

3. **Practice Proper Seed Saving Techniques**

The way you collect and store seeds significantly impacts their vitality. Follow these best practices for seed saving:

- **Harvest at Peak Maturity:** Collect seeds from plants at their peak maturity. This ensures that the seeds have developed fully and are ready for storage.
- **Clean Seeds Thoroughly:** As mentioned in a previous section, properly clean the seeds to remove any plant debris, as this can promote mold or pests.
- **Dry Seeds Adequately:** Ensure that the seeds are thoroughly dry before storing them. Incomplete drying can lead to mold growth and reduced vitality.
- **Store in Cool, Dry, and Dark Conditions:** Maintain seeds in a cool, dark, and dry environment to prevent them from becoming dormant or losing vitality.

4. Maintain Records

Keeping detailed records of your seed-saving efforts is a secret to preserving seed vitality. This practice allows you to track the success of different varieties and ensures you don't forget essential details. Record the following:

- **Variety Names:** Document the names of the plant varieties you're growing and saving seeds from.
- **Harvest Dates:** Note the dates when you collected the seeds. This helps you gauge their age.
- **Isolation Practices:** Keep records of how you isolated plants to prevent cross-pollination.
- **Seed Storage Details:** Include information about where and how you stored the seeds.
- **Germination Rates:** After a period, test the germination rates of your stored seeds to ensure their viability.
- **Successes and Failures:** Don't shy away from documenting both successful and unsuccessful attempts at seed saving. This information can help you learn from your experiences.

5. Encourage Biodiversity

A diverse garden is a healthy garden. Biodiversity strengthens ecosystems and promotes natural pest control while also enhancing seed vitality. Here's how to encourage biodiversity in your garden:

- **Plant a Variety of Species:** Cultivate a wide range of plant species in your garden. This diversity attracts a broader spectrum of beneficial insects and pollinators.
- **Support Native Plants:** Incorporate native plant species into your garden design. They are well-suited to your local climate and can contribute to seed banks for conservation.
- **Create Habitats:** Design your garden to provide habitats for wildlife, such as birdhouses, bee-friendly plants, and water sources.

6. Share and Exchange Seeds

Seed sharing and exchange is a powerful secret to preserving seed vitality. By participating in local seed exchanges or sharing seeds with fellow gardeners, you contribute to maintaining genetic diversity and promoting healthy seeds. Consider these steps:

- **Join a Seed Library:** Many communities have seed libraries where you can borrow seeds, grow them, save some, and return the saved seeds to the library for others to use.
- **Participate in Seed Swaps:** Attend local seed swaps or exchanges to diversify your seed collection and engage with other like-minded gardeners.
- **Connect with Gardeners:** Form connections with other gardeners and exchange seeds informally to broaden the genetic diversity in your garden.

7. **Embrace Organic and Sustainable Gardening Practices**

Preserving seed vitality goes hand in hand with sustainable and organic gardening practices. By prioritizing the health of your soil, minimizing pesticide use, and using natural fertilizers, you create an environment where seeds can thrive. Embrace these sustainable practices:

- **Composting:** Recycle plant waste and kitchen scraps into compost to enrich your soil naturally.
- **Crop Rotation:** Change the location of crops each season to reduce the risk of soilborne diseases and improve soil health.
- **Integrated Pest Management (IPM):** Use IPM techniques to minimize the use of chemical pesticides and prioritize natural pest control methods.
- **Cover Cropping:** Plant cover crops during the off-season to improve soil structure and add nutrients to the soil.
- **Soil Testing:** Regularly test your soil to assess nutrient levels and pH, and amend it as needed.

8. **Continue Learning**

The final secret to preserving seed vitality is a commitment to continuous learning. Gardening is a dynamic and ever-evolving journey. Stay informed about the latest practices, develop your skills, and never stop exploring new ways to improve your garden and conserve seed vitality.

- **Join Gardening Organizations:** Many gardening organizations offer resources, workshops, and educational opportunities for gardeners at all levels.
- **Read Books and Journals:** Stay updated with gardening literature and journals to access valuable insights and techniques.

- **Attend Workshops and Conferences:** Participate in gardening workshops, seminars, and conferences to learn from experienced gardeners and experts.

PART 6

Rebirth - Sowing

Sowing the preserved seeds marks the beginning of a new cycle in your gardening journey. This section will guide you through the process of understanding the optimal timing and techniques for planting preserved seeds, as well as the essential practices for caring and nurturing your growing plants.

Following the Seasons: When and How to Plant Preserved Seeds

Preserving seeds is only the first step in a gardener's journey towards sustainability. The next crucial phase is planting those seeds at the right time and in the right way to ensure a successful garden. Understanding your local climate, the specific requirements of the plants you're growing, and the cycles of nature is essential for effective seed sowing.

1. **Know Your Growing Zone**

Every region has a unique climate, and understanding your local growing zone is the first step in determining when to plant your preserved seeds. The USDA Plant Hardiness Zone Map is a valuable resource for gardeners in the United States, while similar maps are available for other regions. Identify your growing zone, as it will help you choose the right planting times and suitable plant varieties.

2. **Choose the Right Season**

Plants have specific growing seasons, and choosing the right time to plant your seeds is crucial. Here's a breakdown of the seasons and when to plant your preserved seeds:

51

- **Spring:** Many vegetable crops, such as tomatoes, peppers, cucumbers, and beans, are typically sown in the spring when the risk of frost has passed, and the soil has warmed up. Early spring is also an ideal time for cool-season crops like lettuce, spinach, and peas.
- **Summer:** Some heat-loving crops like corn, melons, and okra are planted in the early summer when the soil is consistently warm. If you have a short growing season, starting these seeds indoors and transplanting them can help ensure a harvest.
- **Fall:** In regions with mild winters, you can plant a second round of cool-season crops like carrots, beets, and kale in late summer or early fall. These crops can be harvested well into winter.
- **Winter:** In temperate climates, some hardy varieties of vegetables and herbs can be sown directly in the garden in late fall or early winter. While growth may slow during the coldest months, these plants can still thrive and provide fresh produce.

3. **Plan Your Planting Calendar**

A planting calendar is a valuable tool to help you determine when to sow your preserved seeds. Here's how to create a basic planting calendar:

- **Make a List:** List the plant varieties you want to grow, including their recommended planting dates and days to maturity.
- **Work Backwards:** Start with your region's average last frost date in the spring. Use this date as a reference point and work backward to determine when to sow seeds indoors or directly in the garden.
- **Consider Succession Planting:** Some crops can be planted multiple times throughout the season to extend the harvest. Plan successive plantings to ensure a continuous supply of fresh produce.
- **Include Fall Planting:** If you plan to plant a fall or winter garden, identify the best dates for sowing seeds for these crops as well.

4. **Indoor vs. Outdoor Sowing**

Certain plant varieties benefit from being started indoors, while others thrive when sown directly in the garden. Here's how to decide which method is best for your preserved seeds:

- **Indoor Sowing:** Start seeds indoors for plants that require a longer growing season, like tomatoes and peppers. This method allows you to get a head start on the season. Utilize seed trays or pots filled with seed-starting mix, ensure proper moisture and light, and transfer the seedlings to the garden when the weather becomes warmer.

- **Direct Sowing:** Some plants, like beans, squash, and radishes, can be sown directly in the garden. Choose a location with the right soil temperature, and plant your seeds at the appropriate depth and spacing. Be sure to follow the recommendations on the seed packets for each specific plant.

5. **Prepare the Soil**

The quality of your garden's soil is a significant factor in successful seed sowing. Ensure your garden beds have the right conditions for plant growth:

- **Soil Testing:** Conduct a soil test to assess the pH, nutrient levels, and any deficiencies or imbalances in your soil. Amend the soil as needed to create a fertile and balanced growing medium.
- **Prepare Garden Beds:** Clear the garden bed of debris and weeds. Loosen the soil using a fork or tiller to create a crumbly texture, making it easier for young roots to penetrate.
- **Compost and Mulch:** Incorporate organic matter like compost into the soil to enrich it with nutrients. Apply mulch on the soil surface to retain moisture and suppress weeds.

6. **Follow Proper Plant Spacing and Depth**

Planting depth and spacing are critical factors in ensuring your preserved seeds germinate and grow well:

- **Planting Depth:** Check the seed packet for each plant variety to determine the appropriate planting depth. Some seeds should be sown shallowly, while others require deeper planting.
- **Planting Spacing:** Adequate spacing between plants is essential for good air circulation, reducing the risk of disease and ensuring that each plant has room to grow. Adhere to the spacing guidelines provided on the seed packet for proper plant placement.

7. **Watering and Care**

Young seedlings are delicate, and proper care is essential for their survival and growth:

- **Watering:** Maintain consistent soil moisture without overwatering. Utilize a gentle spray or a soaker hose to prevent disruption to the seeds or seedlings.

- **Thinning:** If you've sown multiple seeds in the same spot, thin the seedlings once they emerge to ensure they have adequate space to grow.
- **Fertilization:** Apply organic fertilizers or compost tea as needed to provide essential nutrients for plant growth. Be cautious not to over-fertilize, as this can harm plants.

8. Pest and Disease Management

Gardens can attract pests and diseases that threaten your plants. Keep an eye out for any issues and take action to protect your garden:

- **Companion Planting:** Planting certain species together can help deter pests naturally. Research companion planting strategies for your specific crops.
- **Monitor for Signs of Problems:** Check your plants on a regular basis for any symptoms of ailment or infestation. The ability to intervene quickly thanks to earlier detection.
- **Organic Pest Control:** Use natural methods to control pests, such as introducing beneficial insects, like ladybugs, or using organic pesticides as a last resort.
- **Crop Rotation:** Rotate crops each season to minimize the risk of soilborne diseases and pests building up in the soil.

9. Label and Record Keeping

To maintain an organized garden and ensure you know what you've planted where, use labels and maintain accurate records:

- **Plant Labels:** Use plant labels or tags to mark the plants in your garden. Include the plant name, variety, and planting date.
- **Record Keeping:** Keep a gardening journal or spreadsheet to track your planting dates, varieties, and any issues or successes you encounter during the season.

10. Embrace Patience and Observation

Gardening is a practice that requires patience and keen observation. Allow your garden to develop, learn from your experiences, and make adjustments as needed. Nature will often provide cues and feedback on how to care for your plants.

Care and Nourishment: Monitoring Growth and Ensuring Plant Health

Once your seeds have germinated and young plants have emerged, your role as a gardener shifts from sowing to nurturing. To promote robust growth and ensure the health of your plants, you'll need to monitor their progress and provide the care and nourishment they require.

1. **Regular Inspection**

Regular inspection of your garden is a fundamental practice to ensure plant health. By observing your plants closely, you can catch issues early and take proactive measures. Here's what to look for:

- **Pest Damage:** Check for signs of pests, such as chewed leaves, holes, or discolored areas. Different pests leave distinctive marks.
- **Disease Symptoms:** Look for signs of disease, such as spots, wilting, yellowing, or unusual growth patterns.
- **Weed Growth:** Keep an eye on weed development, as they can compete for resources and host pests.
- **Nutrient Deficiencies:** Pay attention to any signs of nutrient deficiencies, like yellowing leaves (indicative of a nitrogen deficiency) or discolored leaf edges (indicative of a potassium deficiency).

2. **Watering**

Proper watering is essential for plant health. The right amount of water ensures that your plants receive the necessary hydration and nutrients. Here are some watering tips:

- **Water at the Root Zone:** Water the plants directly at their base to prevent wetting the foliage, as this can potentially result in disease.
- **Deep Watering:** Giving the soil a good soaking can foster deeper root development. A shallow watering pattern might lead to roots that are similarly shallow and fragile.
- **Consistency:** Water consistently, aiming to maintain a uniform level of moisture. Prevent the soil from becoming excessively dry or waterlogged.
- **Morning Watering:** Watering in the morning allows the plants to dry before evening, reducing the risk of fungal diseases.

3. Fertilization

Plants require a balance of essential nutrients to thrive. Soil testing and observation can guide your fertilization practices:

- **Soil Testing:** Conduct soil testing to figure out the quantities of nutrients and the pH of the soil. In light of the findings, fertilizers and other forms of organic matter should be added to the soil as necessary.
- **Organic Fertilizers:** Use organic fertilizers like compost, well-rotted manure, and organic amendments to enrich the soil with essential nutrients.
- **Feeding Schedule:** Develop a feeding schedule based on the specific nutrient requirements of your plants. Different crops may need varying nutrient ratios at different growth stages.

4. Pruning and Deadheading

Pruning and deadheading are essential practices for controlling plant growth and promoting flowering:

- **Pruning:** Trim back overgrown branches and stems to maintain the shape and size of your plants. Pruning also encourages new growth and improves air circulation.
- **Deadheading:** Remove spent flowers to stimulate the production of new blooms and prevent plants from putting energy into seed production.

5. Support and Staking

Some plants, especially tall or vining varieties, may require support to prevent damage from heavy fruits or strong winds:

- **Staking:** Use stakes to support tall plants and prevent them from toppling over. Tie the plants gently to the stakes using soft ties or twine.
- **Cages:** For vining plants like tomatoes, consider using cages to provide support and structure.

6. Mulching

Mulching has numerous benefits for your garden, including conserving moisture, regulating soil temperature, and suppressing weeds:

- **Mulch Type:** Use organic mulch, such as straw, wood chips, or compost, to retain moisture and add nutrients to the soil as it breaks down.

- **Weed Control:** A layer of mulch helps suppress weed growth, reducing competition for resources.
- **Soil Temperature:** The temperature of the soil can be regulated by mulch, making it both colder in the summer and warmer in the winter.

7. Pest Management

Pest management is a critical component of plant care. Organic and sustainable pest control methods are preferred:

- **Companion Planting:** Plant companion crops that deter pests or attract beneficial insects. For example, marigolds can deter nematodes, while dill and fennel attract beneficial insects.
- **Organic Pesticides:** Use organic pesticides sparingly and as a last resort. Options include neem oil, insecticidal soap, and diatomaceous earth.
- **Hand Picking:** For larger pests like caterpillars or beetles, handpick them from your plants and remove them from the garden.

8. Disease Prevention

Preventing diseases is more effective than treating them once they occur. Here's how to minimize the risk of plant diseases:

- **Spacing:** Plant your crops with adequate spacing to ensure good air circulation, which can reduce humidity and the likelihood of fungal diseases.
- **Cleanliness:** Keep your garden clean by removing dead plant material, fallen leaves, and debris, which can harbor diseases.
- **Watering Practices:** Water at the base of the plants and avoid wetting the foliage to reduce the risk of fungal diseases.
- **Crop Rotation:** Rotate your crops each season to minimize the buildup of soilborne diseases.

9. Beneficial Insects

Beneficial insects like ladybugs, parasitic wasps, and pollinators serve a crucial role in preserving a thriving garden:

- **Plant Pollinator-Friendly Flowers:** Include a variety of flowers that attract bees, butterflies, and other pollinators to support healthy plant growth.
- **Avoid Broad-Spectrum Pesticides:** Refrain from using pesticides that harm beneficial insects. Instead, opt for targeted solutions.

- **Provide Habitat:** Create habitats for beneficial insects by adding native plants, nesting materials, and water sources to your garden.

10. **Record Keeping**

Maintaining records of your garden's development is not only a helpful practice but also a way to improve your gardening skills over time:

- **Planting Dates:** Keep a record of when you sowed or transplanted your plants.
- **Observations:** Document your observations, including pest and disease encounters, weather patterns, and any changes you make in your garden.
- **Successes and Failures:** Note what worked and what didn't. This information can guide your future gardening efforts.

11. **Respect Nature's Timing**

Remember that plant growth takes time, and some things are beyond your control. Be patient and respect the natural timing of your garden's development. Understand that not every plant will thrive, but with care and observation, you can create a vibrant and productive garden.

PART 7

Overcoming Obstacles - Tips and Tricks

As you embark on your journey of seed conservation and sustainable gardening, you may encounter various challenges along the way. Here, we will provide you with valuable tips and tricks to help you navigate common seed conservation problems and find solutions. Additionally, we'll share motivational strategies to keep your passion for gardening and conservation alive, even in the face of adversity.

Common Seed Conservation Problems and Solutions

Seed conservation is a critical aspect of sustainable gardening, ensuring the preservation of plant diversity and the ability to grow healthy crops year after year. However, like any gardening endeavor, seed conservation can face challenges that may impact seed quality and viability.

1. **Cross-Pollination**

Cross-pollination occurs when two related plant varieties in the same species, such as two different types of tomatoes, pollinate each other, leading to hybrid seeds and potentially compromising genetic purity.

- Isolation Distances: Plant different varieties with specific isolation distances to prevent cross-pollination. This involves keeping plant varieties far enough apart so that they don't exchange pollen.

- Hand-Pollination: For species with high cross-pollination rates, you can use hand-pollination to control which plants cross-pollinate with each other. Cover the flowers with a bag before they open and transfer pollen manually to the stigma.
- Choose Self-Pollinating Varieties: Opt for self-pollinating or non-hybrid plant varieties that are less prone to cross-pollination.

2. **Seed Storage Issues**

Improper storage can lead to seeds losing their viability, rendering them useless for future planting.

- Airtight Containers: Store seeds in airtight containers to protect them from moisture, pests, and air. Mason jars or specialized seed storage containers work well.
- Moisture Control: Add silica gel packets or rice to the storage containers to maintain an optimal moisture level for the seeds. Excess moisture can lead to mold or seed germination.
- Cool and Dark Location: Keep seeds in a cool, dark, and dry place, ideally at temperatures around 40°F (4°C), to prolong their shelf life.
- Labeling: Clearly label your seed containers with the name of the seed variety and the date of collection to keep track of their age.

3. **Seed Viability**

Over time, seed viability can decline, and it's crucial to determine if the stored seeds are still viable for planting.

- Germination Test: Periodically conduct germination tests to check the viability of your seeds. Place a sample of seeds between damp paper towels and observe their germination rate over a set period, usually a week or two.
- Keep Records: Maintain records of the germination rates of your seeds to ensure you use the most viable seeds in your garden.
- Rotate Seeds: Use older seeds before newer ones to ensure you're always working with the freshest and most viable seeds.

4. **Pest and Disease Damage**

Pests and diseases can damage stored seeds, rendering them unusable for future planting.

- Proper Cleaning: Thoroughly clean seeds before storage to remove any potential contaminants or insect eggs.
- Freezing: Store seeds in the freezer for a few days before sealing them in containers. This can help kill any potential pests.
- Maintain a Clean Storage Area: Keep the storage area clean to prevent pests from infesting the stored seeds.
- Use Pest-Repellent Herbs: Some herbs like bay leaves or neem leaves can act as natural pest repellents in your seed storage containers.

5. Temperature Fluctuations

Fluctuating temperatures in the seed storage area can shorten the seeds' shelf life.

- Consistent Temperatures: Store seeds in a location with stable temperatures, ideally around 40°F (4°C) or slightly cooler.
- Avoid Freezing: While cold storage is essential, avoid freezing seeds, as some varieties may be sensitive to extremely low temperatures.
- Insulate Storage: If your storage area is subject to temperature fluctuations, consider insulating the storage containers with additional layers, like coolers or boxes.

6. Unintentional Hybridization

Sometimes, cross-pollination can occur without your knowledge, leading to unintentional hybridization.

- Isolation and Hand-Pollination: Continue practicing isolation and hand-pollination techniques to minimize the chances of cross-pollination. Be vigilant and observant in your garden.
- Genetic Testing: If you're concerned about the genetic integrity of your seeds, consider investing in genetic testing services that can confirm the purity of your seed stock.

7. Inadequate Labeling

Without proper labeling, it's easy to mix up or lose track of your seed varieties.

- Label Every Container: Label each seed container with the name of the seed variety and the date it was collected. Use waterproof markers or labels to ensure they remain legible.
- Maintain Detailed Records: In addition to labeling, keep detailed records of your seed collection, storage, and planting dates in a garden journal or spreadsheet.

8. Seed Degeneration

Over time, some seeds may lose their vigor and adaptability.

- Seed Renewal: Periodically replenish your seed stock with fresh seeds from the original source or by saving seeds from your healthiest plants.
- Select for Vigor: When saving seeds, choose those from the healthiest and most robust plants. This natural selection can improve the overall quality of your seed stock over time.

9. Poor Seed Harvest

A poor seed harvest can limit the number of seeds you can preserve for future planting.

- Optimal Timing: Harvest seeds when they are fully mature and dry on the plant. Different plants have various signs of maturity, such as dry pods or fruits, browned seeds, or natural seed shedding.
- Gather Seed Pods: Collect seed pods before they shatter, and place them in a paper bag or envelope to capture any seeds that might be released.

10. Inadequate Knowledge

Lack of knowledge about seed conservation practices can lead to mistakes and unsuccessful efforts.

- Continue Learning: Gardening is a continual learning process. Invest time in reading books, attending workshops, and joining gardening communities to gain knowledge and practical skills.
- Seek Mentorship: Find experienced gardeners or seed savers who can provide guidance and share their experiences.

Keeping the Passion Alive: Motivational Strategies

Gardening is a fulfilling and rewarding endeavor, but like any passion, it can face periods of stagnation or burnout. Whether you're a seasoned gardener or just starting out, maintaining your motivation and enthusiasm is essential for a successful and enjoyable garden.

1. Set Clear Goals and Objectives

One of the most effective ways to stay motivated in your garden is to have clear goals and objectives. Define what you want to achieve in your garden, whether it's growing your own vegetables, creating a beautiful flower bed, or contributing to local biodiversity. When you have specific goals in mind, you'll find more purpose in your gardening efforts.

2. Embrace New Challenges

Gardening is an ever-evolving journey, and it's essential to embrace new challenges to keep the passion alive. Try growing unfamiliar plant varieties, experiment with different gardening techniques, or tackle a new landscaping project. These challenges can invigorate your gardening experience and provide a sense of accomplishment.

3. Connect with Fellow Gardeners

Joining a community of fellow gardeners is an excellent way to stay motivated. Whether you participate in local gardening clubs, attend workshops, or engage in online gardening forums, connecting with like-minded individuals allows you to share experiences, gain insights, and find inspiration. Gardeners are a passionate and supportive community, and their enthusiasm can be contagious.

4. Keep a Garden Journal

Maintaining a garden journal is a practical and motivational tool. Document your gardening journey, noting your successes, challenges, and the changes you make in your garden. A journal helps you track your progress and provides a sense of accomplishment as you see how your garden evolves over time.

5. Educate Yourself Continuously

Learning and expanding your knowledge about gardening can be a powerful motivator. Read gardening books, attend workshops, take online courses, and keep up with the latest gardening trends and practices. The more you know, the more confident and inspired you'll become in your garden.

6. Garden for Wildlife

Transforming your garden into a haven for wildlife can be highly motivating. Planting native species, providing water sources, and creating habitat for birds, butterflies, and other creatures can make your garden a thriving ecosystem. Observing the wildlife that visits your garden can be a source of endless fascination and inspiration.

7. Break Down Tasks

Large gardening projects can sometimes feel overwhelming and lead to a loss of motivation. To counter this, break down your tasks into manageable steps. Set achievable goals for each day or weekend, which will give you a sense of accomplishment and keep you motivated as you see progress.

8. Celebrate Small Wins

Celebrate the small victories in your garden. Whether it's the first seedling to sprout, a beautifully blooming flower, or a perfect harvest, take the time to acknowledge and savor these achievements. Recognizing your successes, no matter how minor, can boost your motivation and enthusiasm.

9. Change Your Garden's Design

If you're feeling stagnant in your garden, consider redesigning it. Alter the layout, add new elements, or experiment with different themes. A fresh perspective and a renewed sense of creativity can reignite your passion for gardening.

10. Practice Mindfulness in the Garden

Gardening provides a perfect opportunity to practice mindfulness and be present in the moment. Pay close attention to the textures, scents, and sounds in your garden. By immersing yourself in the sensory experience of gardening, you can reduce stress and reignite your passion.

11. Take Breaks When Needed

Sometimes, motivation wanes because you're overexerting yourself. It's essential to recognize when you need a break. Stepping away from the garden for a short time can refresh your perspective and renew your enthusiasm when you return.

12. Share Your Garden with Others

Invite friends and family to enjoy your garden with you. Sharing the beauty and the fruits of your labor can be motivating, especially when you see the joy it brings to others.

13. Seasonal Adjustments

Different seasons bring new opportunities and challenges. Embrace the changing seasons and adjust your gardening activities accordingly. This adaptability can keep your interest alive as you anticipate the unique experiences each season offers.

14. Set a Garden Budget

Creating a budget for your garden can add an extra layer of motivation. It forces you to make thoughtful choices, research your options, and invest your resources wisely. Working within a budget can inspire creativity and resourcefulness in your gardening efforts.

15. Join Gardening Challenges

Participating in gardening challenges or competitions can provide the motivation to strive for excellence in your garden. Local gardening contests or online challenges often come with recognition and prizes that can keep your passion alive.

16. Experiment with New Techniques

The hobby of gardening is one that is consistently gaining new perspectives, practices, and fashions on on an ongoing basis. Experimenting with these innovations can be an exciting way to rekindle your passion for gardening. Whether it's trying no-till gardening, vertical gardening, or hydroponics, learning and implementing new methods can keep things fresh.

17. Set up a Garden Corner for Relaxation

Create a tranquil corner in your garden where you can relax, unwind, and reflect. Having a peaceful space within your garden can encourage you to spend more time there and enjoy the benefits of your hard work.

18. Invite Inspiration from Other Gardens

Visiting other gardens, botanical gardens, and arboretums can be a wellspring of inspiration. The beauty and diversity you encounter can rekindle your love for gardening and offer fresh ideas for your own space.

19. Tackle a DIY Project

Undertaking a DIY garden project, like building raised beds, creating garden art, or constructing a pergola, can inject fresh excitement into your gardening routine. Completing a project can provide a tangible sense of accomplishment and an increased sense of motivation.

20. Be Patient and Forgiving

Gardening teaches patience and resilience. Understand that not every gardening season will be perfect, and there will be challenges along the way. Be forgiving of yourself and your garden. Learn from mistakes and view them as opportunities to grow and improve.

PART 8

Growing Together - Building a Community

In the world of seed saving, community plays a vital role in the preservation and promotion of crop diversity. Beyond the confines of our own gardens, the concept of building a community of like-minded enthusiasts is fundamental to the long-term success of the practice. In this chapter, we'll explore the importance of these communities, how to discover existing ones, and the benefits of actively participating in them.

Beyond the Garden: Discovering and Creating Enthusiast Communities

Gardening, especially when focused on seed saving, can often be seen as a solitary activity. Many gardeners, initially drawn to this practice by their love of nature and solitude, find themselves on a journey that naturally leads them towards building connections with fellow enthusiasts. Whether you are a seasoned seed saver or just starting out, the joy of finding a community that shares your passion is unparalleled.

One of the first steps in building a community of seed savers is to discover existing groups and organizations dedicated to the cause. These communities can take various forms, from local gardening clubs and online forums to regional seed exchange events and global seed-saving networks. Here's how to get started:

- **Local Gardening Clubs**

Local gardening clubs often host regular meetings, workshops, and events, creating opportunities for like-minded individuals to connect. Joining a club in your area can be a great way to meet fellow seed savers and exchange knowledge. These clubs may have specific interest groups or newsletters dedicated to seed saving, making it easier to connect with enthusiasts who share your passion.

- **Online Forums and Social Media Groups**

The internet has made it easier than ever to find and connect with seed-saving enthusiasts worldwide. Joining online forums and social media groups dedicated to gardening and seed saving can open up a wealth of knowledge and connections. Platforms like Facebook, Reddit, and specialized gardening forums are excellent places to start. These spaces provide a virtual community where members share experiences, ask questions, and offer advice.

- **Regional Seed Exchanges**

Many regions host seed exchange events where gardeners come together to swap seeds and share their experiences. These events often take place in the spring or early growing season and provide a fantastic opportunity to meet local seed savers. Attending these events not only expands your seed collection but also introduces you to a thriving local community of like-minded individuals.

- **Global Seed-Saving Networks**

There are global organizations dedicated to seed saving, like the Seed Savers Exchange in the United States and the Navdanya seed bank in India. These organizations often have members and chapters worldwide, providing an opportunity to engage with a broader, international community. While you may not have the chance to meet every member in person, these organizations often offer resources, newsletters, and online platforms for sharing information and seeds.

Once you've discovered these communities, consider actively participating in them. Attend meetings, workshops, and events, and engage in online discussions. These interactions will not only expand your knowledge but also introduce you to a diverse group of people who share your passion. Here's how to make the most of your participation:

1. **Attend Local Garden Club Meetings**

Gardening clubs frequently host meetings and events throughout the year. Attending these gatherings is an excellent way to meet local seed savers, exchange ideas, and participate in activities related to gardening and seed saving. You might discover unique techniques or varieties that thrive in your local climate.

2. **Contribute to Online Conversations**

Participating in online forums and social media groups can be a convenient way to share your experiences and learn from others. Ask questions, provide answers, and share your successes and challenges. Engaging with the online community can provide a sense of connection, even when you can't meet in person.

3. **Volunteer at Seed Exchange Events**

If your region hosts seed exchange events, consider volunteering to help organize or facilitate these gatherings. It's a great way to become an active member of the local seed-saving community, and you'll get to know other participants better. Plus, contributing your time and energy to such events can be immensely rewarding.

4. **Join Global Networks**

f you're part of a global organization, explore the resources they offer. Many of these organizations have online databases where you can list seeds you have available for exchange. This not only expands your network but also contributes to the broader mission of preserving crop diversity.

Sharing, Learning, and Growing Together

Building a community of seed savers is not just about social connections; it's also about mutual learning and growth. Here are some key benefits of being part of a seed-saving community:

Knowledge Exchange

Within these communities, knowledge flows freely. Gardeners of all skill levels come together to share their experiences, techniques, and tips. Whether you're a beginner looking for advice on seed saving or an experienced gardener seeking new methods, the collective wisdom of the community is invaluable.

As you attend local garden club meetings, contribute to online discussions, and participate in regional or global events, you'll encounter individuals with varying levels of experience. This diversity of knowledge is a treasure trove for those looking to improve their seed-saving skills. You may discover time-tested techniques, innovative approaches, or specific advice tailored to your local climate and soil conditions.

Experienced gardeners often have wisdom to share regarding plant varieties that thrive in your region, the best times for planting and harvesting, and how to adapt to local pests and diseases. Beginners, on the other hand, can offer fresh perspectives and enthusiasm, reminding seasoned gardeners of the joy and wonder in each new planting. The exchange of knowledge fosters a sense of shared growth and enthusiasm within the community.

Seed Diversity

The heart of seed saving is the preservation of crop diversity. Being part of a community of seed savers allows you to access a wide variety of plant varieties, many of which you might not have encountered otherwise. This diversity is not only exciting but also contributes to the preservation of rare and heirloom seeds.

Seed diversity is a fundamental component of food security. By growing a wide range of plant varieties, you create a buffer against crop failures due to pests, diseases, or adverse weather conditions. In a community of seed savers, members often share their excess seeds, offering you the opportunity to experiment with new and diverse crops. Participating in seed exchanges not only enriches your garden but also plays a crucial role in preserving genetic diversity. Many heirloom and rare plant varieties are on the brink of extinction, threatened by the dominance of a few commercial crops. By growing and sharing these unique varieties within your community, you become a guardian of genetic resources, contributing to the global effort to protect our botanical heritage.

Resilience and Adaptation

In the face of a changing climate and environmental challenges, a diverse seed collection can be a valuable asset. By participating in a community, you increase the resilience of your garden and the broader agricultural ecosystem, as you collectively adapt to new conditions.

As our climate becomes more unpredictable, having a diverse selection of seeds becomes increasingly important. Some plant varieties may be more resistant to drought, while others may thrive in areas with increased rainfall. When you exchange seeds and knowledge within your community, you create a dynamic reservoir of adaptable plant genetics. This enables you and your fellow gardeners to respond more effectively to changing conditions and to support the long-term sustainability of local agriculture.

Adaptation isn't limited to climate-related challenges. Gardeners within a community often collaborate to develop and share new varieties through selective breeding. By cross-pollinating plants to achieve specific traits, such as disease resistance, improved flavor, or better yield, you actively contribute to the development of crops that are better suited to local conditions.

Friendship and Support

Gardening and seed saving can be challenging at times. From dealing with unpredictable weather to troubleshooting pest issues, gardeners face a range of obstacles. Having a network of friends who understand your trials and triumphs can provide emotional support, encouragement, and a sense of belonging.

Within a seed-saving community, you'll encounter individuals who not only share your fervor but have also faced and conquered comparable challenges. These collective experiences foster a strong sense of camaraderie, providing valuable support for navigating the ups and downs of gardening.

Friendships within the community can extend beyond the garden. Many gardeners find that their bonds grow stronger as they collaborate on projects, share meals made from garden produce, and even engage in community service activities related to agriculture. These connections add depth and meaning to your involvement in the world of seed saving.

Promoting Seed Saving

Being part of a community allows you to actively contribute to the promotion of seed saving and sustainable agriculture. Through events, outreach, and educational initiatives, you can help spread the importance of this practice to a wider audience.

By joining your local gardening club, for instance, you may have the opportunity to organize workshops or presentations on seed saving, introducing others to the practice and its benefits. These efforts not only educate the broader community but also serve to create a local network of seed savers.

Community outreach can extend to schools, local markets, and community gardens. Engaging in these activities, you become an ambassador for the cause, sharing the joy of gardening, the importance of seed saving, and the broader mission of sustainable agriculture. Your involvement in outreach and education is a way to give back to your community, inspire future generations, and expand the reach of the seed-saving movement.

Beyond the garden, the community is where the heart of seed saving lies. By discovering and actively participating in enthusiast communities, you not only enrich your gardening experience but also contribute to a global movement that is essential for our planet's well-being. The connections, knowledge, and shared passion within these communities are the keys to preserving crop diversity, nurturing sustainable agriculture, and securing our botanical heritage for the future.

PART 9 - Conclusion

The Journey of the Sustainable Gardener

The journey of a sustainable gardener is a remarkable odyssey filled with discovery, growth, and a profound connection to the Earth. Through this series of guides, we've explored the various facets of sustainable gardening, from choosing the ideal garden space to preserving and growing from saved seeds. We've delved into the challenges and solutions in seed conservation, the art of nurturing plants, and how to maintain motivation and find inspiration within gardening communities.

Sustainable gardening is more than just a pastime; it's a conscious decision to coexist harmoniously with nature and take responsibility for our impact on the environment. It's about cultivating not only plants but also a deep connection to the land and a commitment to preserving biodiversity and the planet's well-being.

As a sustainable gardener, you have embarked on a journey of stewardship, seeking to protect and enrich the Earth for generations to come. You are not just tending to gardens; you are also fostering a community of kindred spirits who share your enthusiasm, principles, and deep affection for the natural world.

An Invitation to Curiosity, Learning, and Sharing

Your journey as a sustainable gardener is an ongoing exploration, a path marked by curiosity, learning, and sharing. Gardening, like life, is a continuous journey of growth and self-discovery. As you care for your garden and connect with fellow enthusiasts, you'll learn not only about plants but also about yourself and the world around you.

Never stop asking questions, seeking new knowledge, and experimenting with different techniques. Share your experiences, whether they are triumphs or challenges, with others in the gardening community. Your shared wisdom and stories become part of the collective knowledge of gardeners, contributing to the collective growth and evolution of sustainable gardening.

Interactive Space: Depicting the Ideal Garden

Let's reflect on the concept of the ideal garden once more. Your ideal garden is a living canvas that evolves with your understanding and connection to the natural world. It is not a fixed image but a reflection of your values, interests, and the changing seasons of your life.

As a sustainable gardener, your ideal garden is a space that aligns with the principles of sustainability, biodiversity, and harmony with nature. It's a place where native plants thrive, where you practice responsible water and resource management, and where you actively contribute to the preservation of plant diversity through seed conservation.

Remember that your ideal garden is not a static destination but a dynamic journey. It's a canvas waiting to be painted with the colors of your care and attention, the brushstrokes of your choices, and the depth of your commitment to the well-being of the planet.

As you cultivate your ideal garden, embrace the ongoing cycle of growth, learning, and adaptation. Continue to be curious, share your experiences, and connect with the gardening community. Your sustainable garden is a living testament to the beauty of coexisting with nature, and your journey is a source of inspiration for others who seek to nurture the Earth and grow in harmony with the world around them.

In the world of sustainable gardening, the canvas is endless, the possibilities are boundless, and the journey is eternal. So, pick up your trowel, nurture your garden, and let the colors of your passion and commitment flourish on the canvas of your ideal garden.

PART 10 - Appendices

Glossary of Terms

Annual: A plant that undergoes its entire life cycle, spanning from germination to seed production, within a single growth season.

Biodiversity: Biodiversity encompasses the diverse array of plant and animal species, their genetic variations, and the ecosystems they inhabit. It plays a critical role in upholding a robust and sustainable environment.

Botanical Garden: A place dedicated to the cultivation, study, and display of a wide range of plant species, often including rare or endangered plants.

Companion Planting: This is a gardening method that involves the strategic planting of various plant species in proximity to one another to promote growth, repel pests, and enhance the overall health of the plants.

Compost: Organic matter, such as decomposed kitchen scraps and yard waste, that is used to enrich and improve soil structure and fertility.

Conservation Easement: A legal pact established between a landowner and a conservation organization to safeguard natural habitats, agricultural land, or other valuable resources situated on the property.

Crop Rotation: This is the practice of cultivating different crops in the same area during successive growing seasons, aimed at mitigating soil depletion, pest management, and enhancing soil fertility.

Dormancy: A state in which seeds, bulbs, or plants temporarily halt growth and metabolic activity in response to adverse environmental conditions until more favorable conditions arise.

Drought-Tolerant: Plant species or varieties that can withstand periods of limited water availability and are adapted to arid or semi-arid conditions.

Endangered Species: Plant or animal species at risk of becoming extinct due to a decline in population, habitat loss, or other threats.

Fertilizer: A substance used on soil or plants to supply vital nutrients, including nitrogen, phosphorus, and potassium, to stimulate and enhance plant growth.

Food Security: The condition in which all individuals in a community have access to a sufficient, safe, and nutritious food supply.

Gene Bank: A facility or institution that preserves and stores plant genetic resources, including seeds, for research and conservation purposes.

Genetic Diversity: The variety of genes present within a population or species, which contributes to adaptation, resilience, and the ability to evolve in response to environmental changes.

Greenhouse: A building with transparent walls & roof, designed to create controlled environmental conditions for the cultivation of plants, including protection from extreme weather. This structure is commonly known as a greenhouse.

Habitat Restoration: The process of renewing, restoring, or creating habitats to support native plant and animal species, often after damage or destruction.

Heirloom Seeds: Seeds from traditional plant varieties that have been passed down through generations and are often prized for their historical & cultural significance.

Heritage Garden: A garden that showcases heirloom or heritage plant varieties, often highlighting their historical and cultural significance.

Hybrid: A plant produced by crossing two genetically different parent plants, often selected for specific traits like disease resistance or increased yield.

Invasive Species: Non-native plants or animals that, when introduced to a new environment, cause harm to native ecosystems, species, or human interests.

Integrated Pest Management (IPM): A sustainable approach to managing pests in agriculture and gardening that combines various pest control methods to minimize damage while reducing environmental impact.

Microclimate: The local climate conditions within a specific area, which may vary from the surrounding environment due to factors like elevation, topography, and vegetation.

Mulch: Material placed on the soil's surface to inhibit weed growth, retain moisture, and regulate soil temperature is known as mulch.

Mulching: The practice of covering the soil surface with a layer of organic or inorganic material (mulch) to conserve soil moisture, regulate temperature, and control weeds.

Native Plant: A plant species that occurs naturally and is indigenous to a specific region or ecosystem.

Organic Gardening: A method of gardening that avoids synthetic pesticides and fertilizers, relying on natural and sustainable practices for soil health and pest management.

Organic Pest Control: The use of natural predators, parasites, and other non-chemical methods to manage pests in a garden or agricultural setting.

Perennial: A plant that lives for more than two years, typically regrowing each spring without the need for replanting.

Permaculture: An ecological design approach that integrates sustainable agriculture, landscape design, and energy efficiency to create harmonious and self-sustaining ecosystems.

Pollinator: An organism, such as a bee, butterfly, or bird, that transfers pollen from one flower to another, facilitating the fertilization and reproduction of plants.

Propagation: The process of generating new plants from seeds, cuttings, or other plant parts.

Scarification: A treatment that involves scratching, nicking, or chemically treating the seed coat to facilitate germination, typically required for seeds with hard shells.

Seed Bank: A facility, institution, or storage system that preserves and protects seeds for future use, research, and conservation.

Seed Coat: The protective outer layer of a seed that shields the embryo and provides resistance to environmental factors.

Soil pH: A measure of the acidity or alkalinity of soil, affecting nutrient availability and plant health. pH values below 7 are acidic, while values above 7 are alkaline.

Stratification: A pre-germination treatment in which seeds are exposed to cold, moist conditions to simulate natural winter conditions, often necessary for germination in some plant species.

PART 11 - FAQ: Frequently Asked Questions and Answers

Gardening and seed conservation are essential practices that foster biodiversity and play a significant role in creating a healthier environment. Here are answers to some of the frequently asked questions regarding seed conservation, sustainable gardening, and related topics.

1. **How do I identify healthy plants for seed conservation and gardening?**

Healthy plants typically have vibrant foliage, sturdy stems, and no signs of diseases or pests. Look for well-developed fruits or seeds when collecting from plants. Avoid collecting from plants that show signs of stress or weakness.

2. **What are the best times to harvest seeds from plants in a garden?**

The ideal time to harvest seeds varies by plant species, but it's generally when the seeds are fully mature and dry. For many plants, this is often in the late summer or early fall when seed heads begin to dry out. Avoid harvesting seeds while they are still green or moist.

3. **What techniques and tools can help with effective seed collection?**

Using hand pruners or scissors, carefully cut seed heads or pods from plants. Place the collected seeds in envelopes or containers, ensuring they are fully dry before sealing them. Label each container with essential information, including the plant species, collection date, and location.

4. What are the secrets to preserving seed vitality for the long term?

Proper storage is essential for preserving seed vitality. Keep seeds dry, cool, and in airtight containers. Regularly check for signs of moisture or mold and replace any containers showing signs of damage or deterioration. For long-term viability, some seeds may need specific conditions like cold stratification or scarification.

5. When and how should I plant preserved seeds (sowing)?

The best time to plant preserved seeds depends on the specific plant species and your local climate. Follow the seed's natural growth cycle, considering factors like frost dates and germination requirements. Refer to planting guidelines for each species and ensure proper soil preparation for optimal germination.

6. How can I monitor plant growth and ensure their health in a sustainable garden?

Regular observation is crucial. Watch for signs of pests, diseases, or nutrient deficiencies and take feasible action, like using organic pest control methods or adjusting watering and feeding routines. Proper mulching and weeding also support plant health.

7. What are common seed conservation problems and their solutions?

Common issues include moisture damage, mold, and seed pests. To combat these problems, ensure that seeds are stored in a dry and airtight environment. Regularly inspect stored seeds for signs of damage or infestation and take action accordingly, including cleaning or discarding affected seeds.

8. How can I stay motivated as a sustainable gardener and seed conservation enthusiast?

Gardening and seed conservation require patience and dedication. Stay motivated by setting achievable goals, connecting with fellow gardeners and conservationists, and celebrating your successes, no matter how small they may seem.

9. **How can I connect with other gardening and conservation enthusiasts in my community?**

You can join local gardening clubs, conservation organizations, or online gardening forums and social media groups to connect with like-minded individuals. Attending gardening and environmental events, workshops, and volunteering with local organizations are also great ways to meet fellow enthusiasts.

10. **How can I involve children in gardening and seed conservation to teach them about the environment?**

Engaging children in gardening and seed conservation is a wonderful way to instill a love for nature. Start by involving them in age-appropriate tasks like planting seeds, caring for plants, and collecting seeds together. Explaining the importance of biodiversity and sustainability can make the learning experience more meaningful for children.

References and Further Study Resources

References:

1. "A Seed Saving Guide: For Gardeners & Farmers" Organic Seed Alliance.

2. "Securing our Food, Forever" Crop Trust.

3. "The Organic Gardener's Handbook of Natural Insect & Disease Control" by Barbara W. Ellis and Fern Marshall Bradley.

4. "The Manual of Seed Saving: Harvesting, Storing, & Sowing Techniques for Vegetables, Herbs, & Fruits" by Andrea Heistinger.

Further Study Resources:

1. International Seed Testing Association (ISTA) - An organization that provides standards for seed testing and promotes seed quality globally. Their website offers valuable resources for seed testing and conservation.

2. Crop Trust - The Crop Trust website provides information on the conservation of crop diversity, including global seed conservation initiatives and resources for seed banks.

3. Native Plant Conservation Campaign - A campaign by the Lady Bird Johnson Wildflower Center that focuses on conserving native plant species. Their website offers information on native plant gardening and conservation.

4. Botanic Gardens Conservation International (BGCI) - BGCI is a global network of botanic gardens that work to conserve and restore plant diversity. Their website offers resources on plant conservation and sustainable gardening.

5. The Xerces Society for Invertebrate Conservation - The Xerces Society provides resources on pollinator conservation, including guidelines for creating pollinator-friendly gardens.

6. The Royal Horticultural Society (RHS) - RHS offers a wealth of information on gardening, including guides on plant conservation, seed saving, and sustainable gardening practices.

Exercises, Reflections, and Personal Note Spaces

Seed conservation and sustainable gardening are not only about practical techniques but also about fostering a deeper connection with nature. Here are some exercises, reflections, and personal note spaces to help you embark on your journey as a seed conservationist and sustainable gardener.

1. **Seed Collection Practice:** Start by collecting seeds from your own garden or local plants. Observe the different shapes, sizes, and structures of seeds. Record your findings in a notebook, including the plant species, date, and location of collection.

2. **Seed Cleaning Challenge:** Select a batch of seeds and practice cleaning them to remove any chaff or debris. This hands-on exercise will help you become proficient in preparing seeds for storage.

3. **Garden Planning:** Sketch a plan for your garden, considering factors like plant placement, sunlight, and watering. This exercise can help you visualize and organize your garden for optimal growth.

4. **Seed Sowing Test:** Experiment with sowing seeds from your collection. Observe their germination and growth, and document the process in your gardening journal.

5. **Composting Practice:** If you're not already composting, start a small compost pile or bin in your garden. Learn the basics of composting and observe how it enriches your soil.

6. **Native Plant Identification:** Identify native plant species in your area and take notes on their characteristics, habitat, and significance for local ecosystems. Understanding native plants is vital for sustainable gardening.

Reflections

1. **Connecting with Nature:** Reflect on your personal connection with nature. What inspired you to become a seed conservationist and sustainable gardener? How does this connection benefit your well-being?

2. **Environmental Impact:** Consider the broader environmental impact of your gardening and seed conservation efforts. How do these practices contribute to a healthier planet and a more sustainable future?

3. **Growth and Patience:** Reflect on the growth and development of plants. What life lessons can you derive from observing the patience and resilience of plants as they grow?

4. **Cycles of Nature:** Ponder the cyclical nature of gardening, from planting seeds to harvesting crops. How do these natural cycles align with the seasons of life and the world around us?

5. **Biodiversity:** Contemplate the significance of biodiversity and its role in maintaining ecosystem health. How can you contribute to preserving and promoting biodiversity in your gardening practices?

Personal notes

My Seed Saving Journal

Date: _____

- Today's Weather: _____
- Garden Observations: _____
- Plants in Bloom: _____
- Seed Harvested: _____
- Seed Storage Notes: _____
- Thoughts and Ideas: _____

6. **Planting Schedule**

Month: _____

- Plant Name: _____
- Seed Type: _____
- Days to Germination: _____
- Notes: _____

7. **Seed Inventory**

- Plant Name: _____
- Seed Source: _____
- Quantity: _____
- Date Collected: _____
- Date Stored: _____
- Location in Storage: _____

8. **Breeding Log**

- Parent Plant A: _____
- Parent Plant B: _____
- Date of Cross-Pollination: _____
- Date of Seed Harvest: _____
- Seedlings Description: _____
- Notes on Cross: _____

9. **Pest and Disease Diary**

Date: _____

- Pest/Disease Type: _____
- Affected Plant: _____
- Treatment Applied: _____
- Effectiveness: _____
- Additional Notes: _____

10. **Favorite Varieties**

- Plant Name: _____
- Why I Love It: _____
- Growing Tips: _____

- Culinary Uses: _____

11. **Garden Layout Sketch**

Date: _____

[Include a rough sketch of your garden with labeled planting areas, seed storage, and other important features.]

12.   **Seed Exchange Wishlist**

- Plant Name: _____
- Desired Varieties: _____
- Notes: _____

13.   **Community Seed Swap Contacts**

- Name: _____
- Email/Phone: _____
- Notes: _____

14.   **Future Garden Ideas**

- Plants to Add: _____
- Design and Layout Concepts: _____
- Inspirations: _____

Good bye, and Thanks

See you next book !

Sophie G. Norring

Made in the USA
Las Vegas, NV
05 April 2024